Diary of Our Fatal Illness

PHOENIX POETS

CHARLES BARDES

Diary of Our Fatal Illness

THE UNIVERSITY OF CHICAGO PRESS

Chicago and London

The University of Chicago Press, Chicago 60637
The University of Chicago Press, Ltd., London
© 2017 by The University of Chicago
Published 2017
Printed in the United States of America

26 25 24 23 22 21 20 19 18 17   1 2 3 4 5

ISBN-13: 978-0-226-46802-0 (paper)
ISBN-13: 978-0-226-46816-7 (e-book)
DOI: 10.7208/chicago/9780226468167.001.0001

Library of Congress Cataloging-in-Publication Data

Names: Bardes, Charles L., 1956– author.
Title: Diary of our fatal illness / Charles Bardes.
Other titles: Phoenix poets.
Description: Chicago ; London : The University of Chicago Press, 2017. |
    Series: Phoenix poets
Identifiers: LCCN 2016039076 | ISBN 9780226468020 (pbk. : alk. paper)
    | ISBN 9780226468167 (e-book)
Subjects: LCSH: Terminally ill parents—Poetry. | Catastrophic illness—
    Psychological aspects—Poetry. | Cancer—Poetry. | Patients—Poetry.
    | Physicians—Poetry. | Medical care—Poetry. | Families of the
    terminally ill—Poetry. | Fathers and sons—Poetry. | Autobiographical
    poetry, American. | LCGFT: Poetry. | Prose poems.
Classification: LCC PS3602.A775265 D53 2017 | DDC 811/.6—dc23 LC
    record available at https://lccn.loc.gov/2016039076
♾ This paper meets the requirements of ANSI/NISO Z39.48-1992
(Permanence of Paper).

To the memory, sacred and profane,
of Charles Robert Bardes,
1927–2010

I felt my self far otherwise through all my limbs, than I
Had been before

Ovid, *Metamorphoses*

Where shall a pious father place his son apprentice
to be instructed in the practice of crossing the seas?

John Woolman, *The Journal*

And even as when most welcome to his children appears the life
of a father who lies in sickness, bearing grievous pains, long while
wasting away, and some cruel god assails him, but then to their joy
the gods free him from his woe, so to Odysseus did the land and the
wood seem welcome; and he swam on, eager to set foot on the land.

Odyssey

This other excellent deed of the Dolphins have I heard and admire. When fell disease and fatal draws nigh to them, they fail not to know it but are aware of the end of life. Then they flee the sea and the wide waters of the deep and come aground on the shallow shores. And there they give up their breath and receive their doom upon the land; that so perchance some mortal man may take pity on the holy messenger of the Shaker of the Earth when he lies low, and cover him with mound of shingle, remembering his gentle friendship; or haply the seething sea herself may hide his body in the sands; nor any of the brood of the sea behold the corse of their lord, nor any foe do despite to his body even in death. Excellence and majesty attend them even when they perish, nor do they shame their glory even when they die.

Oppian, *Halieutica*

Whoopi-ty-aye-oh
Rockin' to and fro
Back in the saddle again.

Ray Whitley and Gene Autry, *Back in the Saddle Again*

ACKNOWLEDGMENTS

No part of this poem has been previously published. I thank the
Bread Loaf Writers' Conferences, where, in 2009, I was the Bernard
DeVoto fellow in nonfiction. My deepest thanks to Tom Sleigh,
Randy Petilos, the University of Chicago Press's readers, the book
team for Phoenix Poets, and to Emma Bardes, John Bardes, and
Barbara Kilpatrick.

One

Disease has bent me like a bow, the string is tensed, soon the arrow will fly.

~

My father said, I don't feel well. The doctor said, Tell me. My father said, My knees hurt, and I don't sleep very well, and I have problems with my blood pressure and my cholesterol and my heartburn, and I pissed blood twice, and I lost weight. The doctor mumbled, Ye gods. My father said, I'm tired. The doctor said, Me too, though not in the same way. When did it begin, and where, and how often, and how bad. My father said, Then and here and always and pretty bad, when I walk or lift or listen or think or rest. The doctor said, Subspecialists for each of these. My father said, What then are you doing, and what good are you. The doctor said, I ask myself the same question.

My father said, I feel old. The doctor said, Did you not know at twenty that someday you would be thirty, and someday fifty, and someday eighty. My father said, Did you foresee always hurting. The doctor said, I imagined turning grey, then white, and feeling sore sometimes, my posture ever erect. My father said, Did you imagine the unsteady gait, the falls and near-falls, the urine-stained trousers, the kindly scorn, the condescension. The doctor said, Nature or disease or divine ordinance. My father said, Has taken away all my pleasures one by one. The doctor said, Till death. My father said, Is welcome.

My father said, pointing, There is the empty place where the elder sat. The doctor said, He was arthritic, deaf, and repetitive. My father said, He is gone.

~

81 yo man with chief complaint "I pissed blood." According to his son, a physician, this first occurred 2 weeks ago. According to the patient, a mainly reliable informant, he also had red-tinged urine six months ago and consulted his son, who said it was nothing.

Past medical history notable for hypertension, diabetes, and hyper-cholesterolemia. He smoked 2 packs of cigarettes daily until age 36, when he changed to a pipe, then stopped altogether at age 63. Drinks alcohol "socially." Retired, worked as an engineer in a manufacturing plant, before then a submarine officer. Married, two sons, the elder a physician, the younger a drifter. Review of systems notable for 10 pound weight loss.

On physical exam, the blood pressure was 128/80, heart rate 76. Exam unremarkable.

Impression: Hematuria, rule out malignancy (bladder, kidney)

Plan: urine cytology, CT, cystoscopy

~

I said to my father, Dad, the biopsy shows cancer. My father said, What does that mean, you're a doctor. I said, It can be treated but not cured, managed but not eradicated. Maybe radiation therapy, maybe chemo.

My father said, I shall row, and the father said, Steadfast.

~

My father stood at the head of the dinner table, raised his glass and offered a toast, Give each man his due and who will escape a whipping. Hamlet

~

The oarsman my father leaned over the gunwale, the boat pitched, the sea roiled, whether from the moon, or the wind, or an earthquake somewhere, or a mass of little fishes, or a flick of the tail of great Leviathan.

~

My mother said, What will happen, what is the prognosis. The doctor said, We'll give him some medicine to shrink the tumor, then repeat the scans, don't worry.

My brother said, the Oracle at Delphi once spoke in verse but then only in prose, and later not at all. Had the god stopped speaking; or did the sibyl no longer reach the godhead; or had the age of metaphor passed.

~

My father said, I shall stand straight and tall like a soldier. I thought but did not say, As you always told your sons, though your posture has bent these many years.

The father said, When the frigate Birkenhead struck a rock, the soldiers stood in rank while the ship went down, allowing, they imagined, that women and children be saved, and inspiring poets to limn ballads memorializing their discipline.

~

81 yo man with recently diagnosed transitional cell bladder cancer,
Stage III A, admitted for neoadjuvant chemotherapy. Plan IV
hydration, then chemotherapy in AM.

~

A man walking down the hall of the hospital hears the long howls
of diseases, like faraway coyotes in the night. They sing each to each,
whether planning their attack or awaiting their someday chance.
They shrill and yelp. He barely makes them out, at first, wondering
if the sound is a motor or a dog or an owl or maybe even some noise
of his own mind's making.

He walks again, yes, canine; no, no household dog, a wild thing,
a disease. Their calls become more distinct. They sound distant but
purposeful.

He pricks up his ears. He is older now. The hills surround his own
place, and each one sounds and resounds the long call of no human
instrument. They begin to call for him. Listen, we are the night's
dogs, and you are ours.

He walks again, and there by the nursing station a rustling of under-
brush draws his attention, a tawny long-legged dog disappears in
a flash. Night falls, and now he does not sleep, listening, unable to
disengage. Hath thee in thrall. The voices are louder.

The circles draws tighter, the howls are closer, and now the animals
show themselves shamelessly and unafraid, though he is now
afraid, and one day the least timid, the one with yellow eyes, runs

forward and nips at his leg, he kicks it away, but another comes
from behind, he kicks again, and now the whole pack barks, one
darting forward, one running back in transient retreat, the whelps
of his neighborhood dogs gone wild and interbred with wolves,
or coyotes, and now one leaps and has him by the neck, he beats
his arms, another brings him down, and now he falls, and now he
rises again, he howls, he slathers, he yelps, he runs, his four legs
bounding uphill, and now he pauses and pants and lifts his head
and stretches his neck and straightens his crooked throat and all
together announce and supplicate the cold lucid night.

~

In the house of sickness strangers enter your room. In the house
of sickness the phone is often left unanswered. Someone makes
the bed while you are still in it. Flowers appear from nowhere,
grow stale but stay gaudy. In the house of sickness it is difficult to
distinguish nurses, technicians, therapists, students, and interns,
so often they look and dress alike. It is difficult to distinguish
belief from doubt, the one from the many, health from disease.
The bed is uncomfortable. The bedrails have bars. Unable to leave,
transfixed, as if some hag had cast a spell. The window looks out
over nothing. Everyone asks how you're feeling. You are brought
some place without knowing how. On a gurney you see only the
ceiling. There is much commotion. Smells are hard to identify
but always bear traces of sweat, urine, and bleach. Illness is not so
ennobling or purifying as you had anticipated when well. You do
not catch up on your reading. You scratch. You look around for
something to look at. You ask and you hesitate to ask. You beg
though you would otherwise never beg. Doctors visit very briefly.
Everyone hurries. Quips fall flat. Metaphors illuminate for only
a minute. Reassurances seem like impertinent one-liners. Which

shall win out, order or disorder. So many songs say my love is far away. Your bottom gets sore. There is ample TV but no music. The news is irrelevant. Nice people do nice things. The people wearing pajamas all look pale. The person who draws your blood tapes the vein but applies no pressure, leaving a large bruise. They say you're getting better when you're not. The moon changes from full to new to full again. They write much about you. Machines beep. You may not eat or drink when you want to. In the house of sickness there is too much juice and too little water. People poke and prod you. Sickness is a full-time job. You can focus on little else. There are not enough blankets. You feel chilled. You feel unable. Your ears follow the footsteps of a tall man who strides down the hall but does not stop at your room. Visitors bringing flowers expect to be smiled at, even by passersby in the corridor. You dream of broken things. The razors are dull and pull your overlong whiskers as if by the roots. The washcloths are rough. Scourge and penance. The bark is peeled, exposing the sapwood. Your years of exercise and abstinence seem pointless. You wait. You do not know how long you will be there. You may see a dead man, maybe for the first time. You may see a man tied in restraints. You may hear a man cry out in pain. You may hear a man shouting, No. Wives and husbands recall their vows. Someone walks who could not walk before. Someone speaks who newly was struck mute.

~

The student said, Your patient seems confused. The doctor said, As you should know, this often happens to an aged man admitted to the hospital, given unfamiliar drugs, and unfamiliar foods, and fasts, and sleeplessness, and then the sun sets and the room grows dark and he loses his orientation. We call the phenomenon sundowning.

The student said, I'm a beginner. The doctor said, Read, ninny.

~

My father's hospital roommate lay in the bed nearer the window.
My people, he said, as his IV pump beeped, ate black bread, and
they drank black wine, and they slew a black goat, and spilled his
blood in the fosse.

He pulled back the curtain separating their spaces. How can a man
so young, he said, examining a pale photograph, Become so old.
How does the youth so seeming hale become so ghastly sick.

~

No experience quite like this, to sleep in a strange bed, and then
to become dully aware, still sedated from last night's tablet, of
movement in the room, a band about the arm, tightening, and next
an abrupt insulting sharp prick as the phlebotomist commits her
morning rounds.

~

The roommate announced his giddy exultation in falling sick,
something at least at last has happened.

The consultant told him, Did you not think that taking ill would
give your life a purpose that it otherwise lacked.

~

The hospital fills with sleeplessness, the insomniacs' carnival, where
each frolics alone.

The nurse paged the intern, Doctor, you need to order a sleeping
pill. She has many years experience, he is a novice.

My father said, Difficult to know whether the sound penetrating my drugged sleep was soft persistent rain, or a distant mechanical pump.

~

My father said, Can anyone get a decent cup of coffee around here.

My father said, How about a drink, just one, just a nip, just a splash, just a guss, just a schluck.

My father said, 'Tis Madness to resist or blame / The force of angry Heavens flame.

My father paused a while and said, I was the first of all my family born in a hospital, and once home my mother hired two wetnurses, sisters, named Apollonia and Kunegunda.

~

My father said, In *Lear* there is a doctor, who says, Our foster nurse of nature is repose, The which he lacks. That to provoke in him Are many simples operative, whose power Will close the eyes of anguish.

~

My father said, Why do the words of other men

Count for me more than my own.

~

81 yo man admitted July 9, 2009 with Stage III A bladder cancer. Received neoadjuvant chemotherapy without incident. Hospitalization complicated by intermittent delirium, most likely "sundowning"

related to medications, sleeplessness, and unfamiliar hospital environs.
Follow-up 2 wk.

~

My father said, The hospital disgorges me home, I am to go home, my own footpaths, my own bed, my own woman and wine, but who there will measure and mark my every heartbeat, and sound the alarm should it go amok, and fix it. And wipe my sore behind.

~

My father said, As the fleet left port, a launch sputtered among us, and on it a brass band played the jaunty lament, Empty Saddles in the Old Corral, and when we returned after two months at sea, the band played anew, Back in the Saddle Again.

My father said, When our ship lay anchored at Piraeus, I dared not go ashore, lest I succumb to folly.

~

My father said, In Naples a steel cable fouled the propeller and would have ended my career, until a skiff rowed up with an old man and his two strong sons. Bargaining with gestures, the ancient donned a worn and doubtful diving suit from the last century, connected by a hose to a long-handled bellows contraption, his only air supply. Over the gunwale he went, and he was down a long time while the young men pumped. Don't stop for a second, I prayed, even to wipe the sweat from your brow, or calamity will double. Finally the old man's head popped up, and then his hands, triumphant, holding a heavy knife in one and a sawn length of cable in the other. The only pay he wanted was the chunk of steel, but we tossed in whiskey and many cartons of cigarettes, having averted the wrath of the Fifth Fleet.

~

When you are sick, healthy acquaintances cross the street as they see you approach, embarrassed by infirmity.

~

81 yo man status post neoadjuvant chemotherapy for Stage III A bladder cancer. Feels reasonably well. Trouble sleeping. Plan radical cystectomy, although he may not fully appreciate what this entails. Perhaps a bit daft.

~

My father said, I have observed two species of doctors, those that feel well and those that feel sick, and the first are proud, regaling the world with their robust constitutions, while the second take alternately strong drink and strong coffee, torpor and acuity.

The doctor said, If you had heeded my advice by pouring kerosene into the swamp to eliminate mosquitoes, such cacophony of frogs, toads, and unknown night sounds need never have disturbed your sleep.

My father said, To read a poem properly you must wake up too early and drink too much coffee, or else stay up too late and drink too much wine. The doctor said, To read a disease is the same, sleepless at either end of the night.

~

The stranger saw a girl, Coronis, they dallied, they lay together, the god rose and went away. Time passed, her belly grew round, she felt lonely and afraid. One of the local boys was nice to her, the girl liked him and took him to bed, but this outraged Apollo, how dare she mix mortal seed with his own, he smote her dead. Yet as the flames rose on her funeral pyre the god pitied his unborn son, freed him from the womb, lifted him up, and named him Asklepios.

Dad, I said, Try to focus.

My father said, You try to focus when you haven't slept in three nights. Pay attention, the boy became the Physician, you bozo, the hero the god of Medicine. Born then, born again and again.

He said, Medicine begins when the god pursues a mortal who weds and then defies him, begetting the first physician, human son of an immortal.

Dad, I said, the gods were long ago, there are no gods.

My father said, Medicine begins when human physicians pierce the boundaries between disease and health, mortals and immortals, necessity and freedom. The act is heroic and blasphemous both, worthy a god's homage, worthy a god's outrage.

He said, The gods are the *athanatoi*, the undying, the deathless, and we by contrast are those who die.

Dad, I said, everyone dies.

~

My brother sent a postcard picturing the buried terracotta army of Qin Shi, the first emperor, who ordered that all Confucian books be burnt, excepting those concerning three subjects, being medicine, agriculture, and divination by tortoises.

~

My mother said, Your father descends underground. He is climbing down a long, deep stairway. Dim bulbs intermittently light the path. He stumbles forward and always downward. He speaks seldom and with little content. He knows the way and does not know the way.

My father said, I think of Odysseus, but there is no Tiresias to receive the sacrifice; of Aeneas, but there is no sibyl; of Dante, but there is no Virgil, no Beatrice, and no reemergence into the light.

My mother said, My husband is become a miner treading incautiously down the deepest tunnels, seeking some ore he never will bring back.

My father said, The shadows on the cave's wall are the same that mark my room. The doctor said, The descent beckons as the ascent beckoned.

My mother said, Still I am lonely and soon will be all alone.

My father said, I knew a dog who, late in her doggy life, dreamed of bounding over hills, herding sheep, and keeping the wolf at bay. I knew a man who, late in life, dreamed of sailing ships, hoisting sails, watching at night, and braving storms. I knew a man who dove a submarine, deeper and deeper, beyond sound and light, beyond any recall.

~

My father said, Naught to be seen but the conning tower, the canny, the cunning, the kenning, the whale road.

~

81 yo man bladder cancer chief complaint "Can't sleep." Rx Zolpidem
5 mg 1–2 qhs PRN. Left leg pain; exam normal, doubt metastasis;
Rx Ibuprofen 400 mg TID. Mit Schlag.

~

My father said, When you visit the doctor you wait a long time.
Your time is not your own. The waiting room is a blank space.
Upholstered chairs shiny with Stain-Guard.

A man burst in, shouting Glass in my foot, a bone in my craw, a
mote in my goddamn eye.

A sick man said, I reached home yesterday just after dusk, and I
stirred the lawn with a stick and caused a score of serpents, or small
mammals, to fly through the wet grass every which way.

A woman retained the busy physician, Your pills, Sir, retard my
evacuations. The doctor said, My lady, your poesies and mine.
She said, Calcium, I believe. He said, Concretions and ossifications.

A man said, My sickness is bunk, spinning his wheelchair around
the corner, over the doorsill and into the doctor's office, And this
chair is bunk, and so is your consultation.

A woman said, My leg became stiff. Then my hand grew clumsy.
This, they said, was Parkinson's disease, paralysis agitans. My friends
became impatient and cannot recognize my former self. They call
less frequently than before and do not enjoy my company.

Another emerged from her visit, paid her bill and walked towards
the door, she said, I kissed and he did not kiss back.

When I finally saw the doctor, I told him how my leg hurts. The doctor said, Femur, patella, tibia, fibula, talus, calcaneus, cuneiforms, metatarsals, and fourteen little phalanges.

~

Some men are interesting only insofar as their wives are beautiful. Or ugly. Some doctors find their patients interesting only insofar as they exhibit exemplary health or exemplary disease.

~

My father said, Health is become a faraway love, like her sung of the Provençal poets.

The receptionist said, There is no faraway love now, we all have cellphones, we text whensoever we will.

My father said, She cannot be approached, whatever my desire, who gives me neither friendship nor accord, and still she shines in splendor, like sunlight in an open window, full of disdain, and I forget myself.

My father said, Heigh ho, would she were mine!

~

It must have been three in the morning when my father phoned. Son, he said, I traveled for days until I reached the center. I underwent purifications and slept in the temple, where incense and fumes wafted through the air, serpents slithered between the supplicants, and priests tiptoed about us. There I learned my cure in divine dreams and snaky whispers.

Dad, I said, Do you know what time it is, I have to work, go back to
sleep.

~

*81 yo man bladder cancer Chief complaint fatigue. Exam normal. PET
scan showed reduction in tumor bulk following neoadjuvant chemo.
Differential diagnosis includes thyroid, B12, hyper/hypoglycemia, sleep
disorder, depression, medication side effect, malignancy, functional.
Check labs. Surgical consult.*

~

My father said, I feel so tired, and yet you say the cancer has shrunk,
What then is my diagnosis. The doctor said, I don't know, it may
be A or B or even C. My father said, But you must know, your
training your tomes your monuments your fees. The doctor said,
Ours is an uncertain science. My father said, The sibyl at Cumae
wrote out her prophecies and stacked the leaves neatly, but what-
ever man entered her cave sent them swirling in gusts in eddies in
miniature cyclones in disorder in disarray.

The doctor said, We'll run some tests.

The technician said, See our magnificent machine. A workman cast it,
and a goldsmith overlaid it with gold.

~

The tree split in two, an old maple, and crushed the car in the drive-
way. It had not been strong, however it appeared, and split in a gentle
rainstorm. The fall woke us from sleep, though the noise was modest,
like an enormous squirrel that leapt through wet leaves.

Nearby bees, disturbed, swarmed from their hive to form a tight ovoid ball, some ten thousand strong. Renegades flew everywhere but did not sting. Some huddled inside, pressing against the windowpanes until they dropped, exhausted, and formed little piles on the sills.

~

81 yo retired naval officer with recently diagnosed Stage III A transitional cell carcinoma of the bladder, significant response to chemotherapy. Prognosis fair. Plan radical cystectomy with cystostomy. Explained need for external bag w/ patient and family. Son is a physician; meddlesome. NPO.

~

Emerging from stupor five days after his surgery, my father opened his eyes and said, In the Great War my father manned anti-aircraft artillery in France, and one day a German plane strafed their position, and he wanted to run, but the corporal couldn't flee in sight of his lieutenant, nor the officer before his man.

~

The surgeon said, For in the past the essence of surgery was speed. His chest swelled, he brandished his instruments. The student watched as he made his incision, cauterized vessels, applied the saw, and completed the amputation. The surgeon said, Thirteen minutes flat, and left. The student received the specimen and dressed the stump. They took the leg to one place, and the patient to another.

~

After her hip surgery, the patient said, The assistants they tell me prepared my leg, made the incision, sawed my bone, next welcomed the great surgeon to insert the prosthesis.

~

My father stood at the toilet. Dad, I said, What are you doing.

Trying to take a leak, he said.

Dad, it doesn't work that way anymore, you had an operation, they took out your bladder, see, the urine comes out in a bag.

What am I then become, he said, a useless appendage, a disjoined progenitor. Pin the tail on the donkey.

~

Morbidity and Mortality Conference

Yesterday the man with pancreatic cancer could not be awakened.
The nurse shouted, summoning a dozen residents who quickly thrust
a breathing tube down his throat, jammed large needles into his veins,
pumped the chest, then shocked the stopped heart, then again. Shouts,
orders, commotion, commentaries, opinions, assessments, judgments.
Students tried to make themselves useful, eager and afraid to watch.
The body jerked convulsively: an epileptic seizure, then another,
then a third. Then the seeming lifeless body was still. Spilt blood was
everywhere. The doctors continued their compressions, and when they
paused a moment, the heart began to beat on its own. A pulse, yes,
returned. Congratulations all around. The man has been saved.

Saved indeed. He will require a breathing tube, a feeding tube,
a bladder tube, and months of hospitalization. Bedsores are likely.
His brain, starved for oxygen those many minutes, will only partly
recover. He may never go home.

~

My father said, Dolphins came to play with the ship, and the worst
blasphemy I ever saw was the man who took a rifle to the foredeck
and shot them.

~

Transfer note

*81 yo man with bladder cancer, Stage III A, diagnosed July 2008,
status post neoadjuvant chemotherapy followed by radical cystectomy
with prostatectomy and cystostomy 10/2/2008. Past medical history
notable for diabetes, presently off medications in setting of weight
loss. Now transferred to subacute rehab. Sometimes confused at night
(sundowning), needs frequent reorientation. Needs encouragement
to eat. Sometimes gabby, sometimes mute for long spells.*

~

What they called the rehab center proves to be more a nursing
home, where certain wings share the smells of pedestrian under-
passes, remote subway platforms, and disused houses of worship.
Fabrics left too long damp, human bodies left too long unwashed,
yeasty brews, an overlay of disinfectant and pesticide. A radiator
clanks. If someone is speaking as you arrive, wait respectfully before
you enter, lest you break the spell.

~

My father turned towards me as I entered the common room,
and a slight shiver crossed the ancient's eyes, his lids rising, for an
instant, his pupils dilating, an instant, before he sank again into
deep fathoms, deep repose, deep silent steadfast bowed absence.

My father bent forward, head near his knees in unholy prayer, he nearly slumped out of his wheelchair, I held him back, Dad, I said, Stand straight and tall like a soldier.

My father said, A little touch of Harry in the night.

~

What do you do for kicks here, the visitor asked the man consigned to rehab after his long pneumonia. Watch the girls, replied the octogenarian. He smiled, he gave the thumbs-up sign. He paused. I feel like dogshit.

~

My father said, They say I must eat. I could go for a month, partake of nothing, and disturb the universe not a whit.

They bid me take jello and fruitdrinks, syrup, blandishments, pap, and sweets.

The hale and youthful sip honey, the sick chew husks and straw.

~

The sick man's feet became hooves, his legs sprouted stiff brown hairs, and then his torso and his arms, his face grew long, antlers sprang from his forehead. He called out, but the voice that emerged was changed, he brayed, and his dogs came running, yelping in glee, fangs bared, they leapt on the great stag, one on his nape, another on his flank, they bit deeper and deeper, tearing his flesh.

The sick man sees the goddess intact, naked, he yells unintelligibly, his hunt's own dogs rip him to pieces. Fatal metamorphosis.

The goddess makes note, disturbed for a moment, then calmly dresses and goes her way.

~

Of a clear afternoon my father and I watched his favorite movies, as often we had before, being Laurence Olivier's Henry the Fifth, and Spencer Tracy's Captains Courageous.

~

The cattle munched their meadow grass, as they had before, and rain began to fall, as it had before, and the next day still it rained, and on the third day still, and the cows went on chewing and swatting flies with their tails, and on the fourth day puddles formed in low places, and on the fifth ponds and creeks overran their banks, and on the sixth the gullies filled with water, so the beasts gathered on higher ground, and still the water rose, until they crowded together there on their hillocks and felt the waves lapping their hoofs, and when the water reached their dewlaps they saw a single huge boat, not too far, its gangplank stowed and its portals sealed shut, floating away, heedless while they bellowed.

~

My father's surgery had gone well enough, considered by itself, but there followed confusion and depression, leading to near starvation, inanition, and a circling towards doom that kept him hospitalized for nearly two months.

From these he was rescued by drugs and support, and total abstinence from drink, for this had been his boon companion for lo these many years. When he returned home, my mother gave him his wine, which the doctors had forbidden, either strictly or

not depending on the auditor's intent, and he began to circle again.
The doctor said, It could kill him. My mother said, We are husband
and wife.

~

The maelstrom, I said. A bullshit legend, said my father, We'd pick
up the rummies by Sailors' Snug Harbor and buy them a drink and
hear their tales, the kraken, the roc, the harpies, the easy girls of
Cadiz, and dog-headed mermaids.

~

Drink, said my father, Once meant the soul's bougainvillea, maypop,
passionfruit, dithyramb, quick-sprung lianas, strangler figs, calamus,
liverwort, Aeolian fronds, ferns ecstatic, but more often, and most
recently, a sodden and stuporous bog.

~

My father said, The truck was speeding and drove off the road and
crashed into a tree and spilt its cargo into the ditch, being words
and snatches, who picked themselves up and ran off into the woods,
jabbering and giggling and yelling like jubilant bonobos.

~

Once back at home my father revisited the family memorabilia
that festooned his private walls, mainly the stairs to the basement.
I steadied his arm. First was the photograph of a victory parade,
where his own father, armed with a sword, led the ranks of men
marching in khaki jodhpurs and boots. Another, nearly four feet
wide, showed the Third Pennsylvania Field Artillery, among them
his uncle Otto, mounted near the Mexican border, preparing to
hunt down banditos. Then came the painting from his grandfather's

butchershop, executed to pay the artist's overdue bill, picturing a fierce eagle that flew across a war-torn sky, its talons clenching ribbons with the names Belleau Wood, Second Marne, and The Argonne, being battles where his father and uncles had fought.

~

The old vets at the VA hospital stayed for weeks and months on end, often indefinitely, as they recuperated from illness or surgery, or awaited an authorization, or did nothing at all. As we made our morning rounds, they watched the overhead TVs, which at that time broadcast new shows with exercise girls in bright lycra body suits gyrating in formation. The otherwise chatty men watched silently, slack-jawed. The head girl, who stood before the others, wore shiny orange-red and called in rhythm *In—Out—Enjoy it!* to the rank and file before her. The interns could not catch the men's attention and often sneaked a peak themselves. The show immediately following was Popeye the Sailor, which fulfilled its hour as the hoarse ancient seaman sang his ditty, sounded his pipe, and puffed out smoke.

~

My father said, I heard the doctor instructing his interns how to avoid unpleasant personal contact: read books, drink wine, fiddle with contrivances, pass the hors d'oeuvres, regard lab results, address mainly the other doctors and nurses. They took careful notes and nodded each to each.

~

My father said, The bucko mate was a burly man who beat the crew with his fists, with a spike, with a rope, and drove them harder and faster, productive and economic, until they dropped from the rigging, exhausted, into the sea.

~

My mother phoned me late Saturday night, saying, Your father
is coughing, and he has a fever. I said, Did you call the doctor.
My mother said, No, I didn't want to bother him, I'm calling you,
you're a doctor, your father trusts you. I said, Does he have runny
nose, sore throat, sneezing, headache, shortness of breath or chest
pain. My mother said, No, yes, no, yes, maybe, no. I said, Sounds
like a virus, give him fluids rest and TLC. My mother said, Are you
sure. I said, Call me if he's not better.

~

*81 yo man with bladder cancer, admitted with fever and cough for
3 days. Chest x-ray shows dense infiltrate right middle lobe. Plan IV
antibiotics and fluids. Watch for cloud-cuckoo land.*

~

My father said, I began to cough, and then I felt hot, and then I
could not catch my breath. I saw the doctor. Breathe. He asked me
questions, Breathe, He held his periscope to my chest, Breathe, he
said I had pneumonia, Breathe, he put me in the hospital.

Dad, you mean stethoscope. Whippersnapper, he said, trying to
catch his breath. He leaned forward and braced his arms on his
knees, the better to suck in air. His lips and fingertips were blue.

My father said, I have crossed the oceans, wondering what it was to
drown.

My father breathed laboriously, my father gasped his several days
despite the oxygen mask. A sailor angles his craft this way and that
to catch the wind, the sail luffs and flaps.

~

My father said, between coughs, They told me sickness refines a
man, rendering me triumphant should I be cured, and stoically
enlightened should I not. How unkind a burden, how unjust
to him who emerges spent, weakened, lame, reduced, damaged,
palsied, less whole, less intact, less able, finally less a man.

~

A doctor walked the halls of the hospital, humming to himself, it
sounded like Elvis's Heartbreak Hotel, but he substituted his own
words, He's got pneumonia, baby, He's got pneumonia, baby, I get
so lonely I could die.

~

My father, nearly recovered, said, I like to think how spirit,
breath, and wind are all the same word. So that the spirit of God
that moves across the water at the Creation could be his breath,
or merely the wind. I like to think how we all inhale and exhale the
same air.

The doctor said, Respiration, inspiration, expiration. My father said,
I like to think on the first breath of a newborn child, and the last
breath of a man who dies.

~

Dad, I said, Do you remember when I was four and a wave knocked
me down and rolled me under I tumbled over and over it seemed
endless, until you reached and pulled me up from the water.

~

My father walked stooped and slow, scanning the sidewalk for coins, sometimes bending to pick up a dime or more often a bottle-cap, crooking his finger into newspaper boxes, vending machines or public phones, hoping for lost change.

~

81 yo man with bladder cancer, recently hospitalized for pneumonia, treated with broad-spectrum antibiotics. Feels well but tired.

Might I not heal by word and hand. Did not the ancients cure by intoning charms, and were these not composed in verse, and was the healer not a poet. Did not the poet bend the cosmos the way a prism bends a ray of light. Does not the word expel disease, invest the amulet, actuate the herb, and avert the curse.

All children fear shots, but in skilled hands the injection hurts less, and in skilled hands the cancer hurts less, and the dread, and the grief, and the parting.

~

In the waiting room I saw a crone grip the doctor's knee, as if to emphasize her point. The physician, though comfortably middle-aged, recoiled from her strong bony fingers, shuddered, and rose to wash his hands. Tonight I saw him run outdoors, lift a stout stick, and beat the crossroads ferociously.

~

A child spotted a dead shape up the road, maybe a possum, and froze and cringed and would walk no farther until his dad, wielding a stick, flipped the carcass into a ditch.

As I walked by a pond three ducks suddenly flapped and skedaddled, though I meant them no harm.

Then geese honked behind reeds, and then a kestrel, empty-taloned, darted quickly away.

~

My father said, The earliest ships had shallow drafts and kept close to shore. To cross the open sea required deeper keels, higher bulwarks, and sail to supplement oars.

~

The doctor said, We have achieved remission. My father said, Does this mean cure. The doctor said, Rather held in check, held at bay, arrested, the wolf is muzzled or leashed, for now. The patient said, Gone. The doctor said, Halted. The patient said, Remission of sins, remitted sentence, am I now freed. The doctor said, A respite, a slackening, reprieved for a short day. The patient said, What were my transgressions. The doctor said, Did you not walk this earth.

~

My father said, Birds seldom are struck by cars, though they dart perilously close. The doctor said, In contradistinction to possums, raccoons, groundhogs and skunks, who munch roadside rubbish.

~

My father said, I dreamed I sailed an open boat across the Antarctic Sea and reached a distant island, where the beach was piled eight feet thick with broken masts, yardarms, decking, timbers, all shipwreck debris, and then again figureheads, cabin doors, carved ornaments, and oars, most of which had drifted a thousand miles or more from Cape Horn and the dire Straits of Magellan.

~

The doctor said, I have a student with me today, I hope you don't mind. My father, meaning to indicate approbation, said, How admirable that you teach. The doctor, meaning to indicate modesty, said, I merely prepare the banquet and invite the students to feast. My father said, Do you admonish gluttony and greed.

~

My father said, Who might these be. The doctor said, I told you, my brilliant students, accomplished if nameless, high scores every one. My father said, So quick bright things come to confusion.

My father said, What are those spots on my brain MRI. The doctor said, We call them UBOs, unidentified bright objects.

~

My father thumbed through the dictionary, Prank, prate, prattle, pravity, praxinoscope.

I interrupted, What's that, Dad. My father said, A scientific toy, like a magic lantern, to create the illusion of action.

My father continued, Next are praxis, pray.

~

My father said, If my brothers or I required correction following some disobedience or prank, our father plunged the miscreant's face into a sink full of water, and held it there until his point was made, having been so advised by the family physician.

He pulled forth our heads, we gasped, breathless, dripping,   daring
not to meet his eyes.

~

My father said, I suffer pain. The doctor said, Where. The patient
said, There. The doctor said, Here, and the patient said, There and
there and there and there. The doctor said, When does it hurt,
and the patient said, When I stand when I bend when I void when
I am touched. The doctor said, How can I help you if the pain is
everywhere, and the patient said, How can you not.

~

Dad, I said, Why do you now read only the history plays. My father
said, When I was young the tragedies were painless, Son, wait, wait
and you shall see.

Two

My father said, There is blood in my urine bag.

The doctor said, Relapse. You will need a second operation.

My father said, Why am I not well, is the rat's hunger never sated.

~

My father said, The creature was small at first, like a lap dog that yipped its way into consciousness; but then it grew, the little digits became claws, the wee kissy mouth a great maw, the pinteeth daggersharp fangs, the tongue slathered, the beast loomed, it roared, commanding every moment's attention.

~

A cat crouched in the grass, a chipmunk perched on a stone wall, they stared each other down. The prey was safe, never more than inches from a crevice. He turned his back, wary, he munched a seed, his cheeks puffed out hamstering something for future meals, he turned again to eye the predator. So secure, defiant, confident, and then he hopped down, going about his business, and the cat pounced, a turmoil, and then trotted the predator, carrying the chipmunk drooped, limp, dangling by his nape.

My father said, I ate sprouts, I abjured red meat, I exercised, I prayed, I harmed no one, why am I again taken ill.

~

Dad, I said, The time for surgery is come again. My father said,
The two hours' traffic of our stage.

~

*82 yo man with bladder cancer, newly metastatic, now Stage IV,
admitted for palliative surgery. Many lab tests, many unnecessary.
Bowel prep, NPO.*

~

Awakening from anesthesia, my father said, The temple stood
beside a chasm. I fasted, abstained from sleep, bathed in the river's
cold waters, and sacrificed a black ram, spilling its blood into the
split earth. I drank from two fountains, Forgetfulness and Memory.
I dreamt. I had been cured. I had unlearned how to laugh.

The hospital, said my father, is a stunned temple. The priests there
take away your clothes and dress you in their sacramental pajamas.
Your drink their waters, descend and re-emerge. Maybe.

~

My father's roommate said, One day my stool was black like tar, and
the doctor said I bled, and the biopsy said cancer, and now I plan
my surgery, for the cunning man will operate tomorrow, and my
son visits from faraway, and my disease will be gone, and with it my
stomach, and I stay cheerful to the end how shall I eat it cannot be.

~

My father went home, once again.

Sputtering brine.

My brother sent a postcard, recto a black bird, verso a script,
Beethoven, String Quartet number 15, Opus 132. A Convalescent's
Holy Song of Thanksgiving to the Deity, in the Lydian Mode. 1825.

~

My father teetered cautiously down the stairs to the basement, his
favorite place, where often after supper he would retreat and tinker,
fixing stuff. Lining the shelves were the yellow cans of Barking
Dog tobacco, from which he once filled his pipe, but which now
held screws, bolts, washers, nuts, assorted nails, and such workshop
impedimenta. Also toy soldiers and small metal cars that once his
sons had treasured, then cast away heedless.

~

My father said, What causes bladder cancer.

Dad, I said, Unless you worked with aniline dyes, I'm sorry, tobacco
and drink.

My father said, I ate eels boiled in broth, and I fain would lie down.

~

The doctor said, The pestilence comes of three things: the root
beneath, the root above, or sometimes both together.

~

My father, as usual, had gone to bed early, but he appeared down-
stairs some hours later, stark naked, bare as the day he was born,
and shriveled, as the newborn sometimes are.

~

My father awoke, dazed and befuddled, he unsheathed his father's cavalry sword, a ceremonial prop from the National Guard, polished steel nearly a yard long, and brandished his weapon to slay the imagined intruder.

~

My father consulted the doctor, saying, I weaken and grow feeble again. The doctor said, Your cancer is back. My father said, Was it ever gone. The doctor said, Verily, no.

The disease was a dog who waited faithfully many years for the long-absent master to return, sniffed, smelled his smell, yapped happily, and licked the beloved familiar hand.

~

82 yeoman metastatic bladder cancer admitted with failure to thrive. Urine in ostomy bag cloudy; suspect infection. Plan: IV antibiotics, ascertain resuscitation status.

~

Remembering his prayers of years before, threescore and ten, my father said, Thou shalt not be afraid for any terror by night; nor for the arrow that flieth by day; Nor for the pestilence that walketh in darkness: nor for the sickness that destroyeth in the noon-day.

~

Feverish, demented, delirious, hey nonny no.

~

Last night my father cocked his ear toward the hospital window and heard the sounds of clashing swords and men yowling their triumph or their anguish.

~

My father said, In the brief trances of the artillery One cry from the
destroyed and the destroyer Rose, and a cloud of desolation wrapt
The unforeseen event.

~

At bullfights the beast falls first to its front knees, which buckle
under the fatal blow, then collapses entirely on the ground. I have
seen dying patients fall the same way, though not on the same knees,
and the toreador struts like a cockatoo.

~

My father said, You read me like a book, sir. The doctor said, But
halfway through I'm really only skimming.

~

My father said, The neighborhood dogs once drove me batty,
yipping, yapping, yelping, growling the postman, barking the
squirrel, howling the moon, and slavering, slobbering, nipping
my trousers, nipping my hand, and fouling my footpaths, chasing
my car, and begetting their own in public places, whelping in
perpetuity, now they welcome me home.

~

My father said, Canis Major, the Great Dog, snaps at the heel of the
hunter.

~

After her stroke, all she could say was Awful, awful, and sometimes
O God. The family thought she meant to say, How very bad it all
is, bemoaning her ills and cursing the world that formed them;

but years later the grand-niece said, Awful once meant amazed, astonished, and full of wonder, so that maybe Aunt Mimi, recalling old authors, found her new mind inspired and bowed before its throne.

~

I changed my father's ostomy bag, I cleansed his soiled trousers, I pried grime from under his nails, I wiped bits of food from his chin's stubble, I steadied him in the shower, seeing his loose flesh sag, I laid him in his bed.

Albany said, How have you known the miseries of your father. Edgar said, By nursing them, my Lord.

~

The doctor said, You must not drink, and the patient said, I must drink, and the doctor said, You suffer depression, which drink shall worsen. The patient said, Whence then my animation, my pleasure, my spiritus, my consolation, my sleep. The doctor said, You must find them elsewhere. The patient said, They are nowhere to be found. And the wife of many years said, Nowhere.

~

The wife said, Don't. The husband said, I shall do as I please. The wife said, It will make you ill. The husband said, So it shall, but you will take care of me. You will spoon me my soup, holding a cloth under my chin to catch the dribbles, you will dress my wounds, you will sponge my brow, you will take my arm, you will walk me, you will wipe my soiled tail. The wife said, So I shall, and the wife thought, I shall not.

~

The inquisitor said, Your husband, newly home after cancer surgery, lay on the floor for three days, too weak to rise, and yet you did not call for help. The wife said, I am not the sort to call the fire brigade for a cat stuck up a tree.

~

One would have thought that the husband and wife, married some sixty years, would, after the accident, have asked first about the other from their separate hospital beds, but both drew too deeply into their own injuries, who once had eyes only for each other.

~

My father said to his disease, I am become your cupbearer, filling your chalice, or pouring out wine to these your many guests.

Who is it walks beside you. Said the patient, My disease.

~

82 yo man widely metastatic bladder cancer, admitted for dehydration and failure to thrive. Rx IV fluids. Looks like his last legs.

Do not thump on his chest Do not break his ribs Do not shock his heart Do not breathe his breaths Do not puncture his throat nor his stomach Do not dialyze his kidneys Do not resuscitate.

~

A woodsman cut the tree a drayer hauled it a sawyer cleaved it a carpenter hewed it then hoisted it overhead and drove the nail home.

~

I sit at my father's bedside, reading. There is little else to do. I seem to keep watch, but watching for what. I am ready to fend off flies and jackals, but these pertain to another time and place. I am ready to respond to any want my father should express, but there is no want. The chest rises and falls. There is no other motion. The slight sound is the passage of oxygen through narrow plastic tubes. My father's doctor enters, speaks some few words, performs some few gestures, and promises some few adjustments.

~

My father said, Soon I shall remove to a faraway planet, and visit you on clear nights.

Galileo, he said, with crude lenses and exceptional eyesight, beheld its four discernible moons.

~

My father said, laboring for breath, How does the earth spin so fast and not a leaf stir.

~

The doctor said, A man nearing death breathes in cycles, a long pause followed by deep quick draughts.

~

My father said, Can't you give me something to bring this to an end. I the physician the son said, No, Dad, I can't.

~

The nurse said, Two logs, smoking beside each other, require only a moment's provocation to desquamate into flame. She paused, and then she said, But later the damn things sputter out anyway.

~

Two doctors met at the nursing station. They chatted and compared their hi-fi systems. One said, The immutable forms. The other, Sonics and acoustics.

~

My father's roommate said, I am glum and cranky. The doctor said, Are you depressed. The patient said, I suppose so. The doctor said, Have you thought of hurting yourself. The patient said, No, but I think of sweeping my arm in a rude, abrupt and graceless gesture across the chessboard, knocking off all the pieces. The doctor said, What of those you love. The patient said, Apparently not enough.

~

The doctor said, There are dogs who would lick their haunches until the fur rubs off, leaving the skin raw and bleeding. To prevent this calamity, veterinarians fashion white plastic cones that fit about the dogs' necks and prevent their turning round. There are boys who scratch their legs, usually about the outside shins, until they too form little sores, which quickly heal, as the young mend quickly, but then the boys pick the scabs, hoping to leave their skin again unmarked, but often needing to staunch fresh blood with pressure from the thumb. Sometimes they perform this exercise at night, staining the bedsheets. The cycle of scratch, bleed, heal, pick, and bleed again can proceed all through the seasons.

There are diabetics for whom such ceremonies cause infection, and sometimes amputation. Some are widows, clean of body, heart, and all.

There was a poet once who said, Let them scratch where it itches.

~

83 yo man with end-stage bladder cancer, admitted for dehydration and failure to thrive. Discharge to home hospice. DNR.

Go, he said, It is finished, return no more.

~

My father said, Damn and bless the hopeful amorous cheer of lightning bugs on hot July nights.

~

Though dressed nicely for the occasion, in navy-blue blazer, pressed shirt, bowtie, and khaki trousers, my father had not properly fastened his ostomy bag, so that urine soaked his pants and corpus, and stank as might be expected.

My father stood as best he could and raised his glass and toasted us all, Might I say, in candor, I am truly glad to be here.

Finally my father, rising from dinner, drank down all the unfinished glasses, even those from others' tables, much dismaying the assembled family, yet his delight.

~

My father said, I will sprinkle clean water upon you, and you shall be clean from all your uncleannesses, and I will remove from your body the heart of stone and give you a heart of flesh.

~

That he suffered from dementia, all agreed, some calling it second childhood, avid for ice cream, though the infant mewls while the man seldom spoke. That he found himself entirely happy, most observers conceded with varying degrees of conviction, for who, some said, could be content settling so idle. The chair sat by a sunny window, and the man sat in the chair, and an orange cat sat in the man's lap.

~

The ancient said, This is not dotage. I am again a seaman, keeping watch, four hours on, four hours off, scanning the sea for disturbances and calms. None so present as I, knowing neither future nor past. If something should happen, I shall report it, and if not all shall be well.

The man in middle age said, My father is become a mariner who, hearing the maelstrom and feeling its pull, draws in his oars and waits.

~

My father said, Poseidon answered to many names, Hippios the horse, Soter the savior, Ennosigaios the earth-shaker, and Asphaleios the steadfast.

And if a man shipwrecked reaches land, The sea had soaked his heart through.

~

My father inclined his ear toward the window and said, In late summer, whatever music you may play, the crickets and cicadas carry the burden.

~

My father said, A man who falls overboard bobs to the surface, but if he struggles and raises his arms he sinks deeper, then pops up again, repeating the cycle two or three times until he rises no more. He gasps and swallows water, which weighs him down. If the water is cold, the chest cannot move, and he neither breathes nor cries out.

The doctor said, The lungs themselves remain rather dry, for the larynx constricts reflexively to close off the windpipe.

My father said, His ears hear dreadful noises, and his eyes behold a thousand men that fishes gnaw upon.

~

My father said, Wouldst thou have me gone.

He said, The eye that mocks a father Will be pecked out by ravens of the valley And eaten by the vultures.

He said, Roman law condemned a man who killed his father to be whipped until he bled, then sewn into a sack together with a dog, a cock, a viper, and an ape, and finally hurled into the sea.

He said, Picture that.

~

My father said, Go not yet hence, bright soul of the sad year.

~

My beloved said, Love and the gracious heart are but one thing.

~

My father said, I rowed and I rowed and I saw a great beast, opening
its maw. My belovèd said, There is a psalm where Leviathan sports
and plays.

~

My father opened his eyes and reported, This, my Lords, was all I
had to say, desiring all your pardons.

~

He merely quenches a dimly burning wick.

~

~

I came to visit my father, the room and its bed were empty, a nurse appeared, Quem quaeris in sepulcro, she said, Whom do you seek in the sepulcher.

~

My brother texted, so Dad is dead.

~

They dragged the slain warrior's body behind a horse, an empty chariot, tearing his flesh and breaking his bones and filling his wounds and mouth with dust, but it mattered nothing to great Hektor, though it mattered to the story, and to Priam, who anyway exists only in my imagination, but also in yours; and I thought on the prince when they burnt the remains of my late father, with little or no ceremony.

~

The celebrant said, The human body does not burn well, requiring intense heat to render it unto ashes. The mighty physician said, he said, In bones well burnt, fire makes a wall against itself.

~

A few days after my father died the images vanished of his suffering, senex, and degradation, and he took up residence in a corner of my mind, where he appeared as he did at fifty, vigorous, lively, and smiling.

A voice said, Like Metis in the mind of Zeus.

The voice said, Metis, yes, measure, and meter.

I hear his voice. A skeptic said, A figment.

~

No thunderbolt struck him down, no whirlwind, no vortex, no war, no sea, rather the dark world split open, glad to receive so wondrous a man.

~

The child reads the father story, page by page, as he imagines them, and none other shall stir these leaves.

~

My father is dancing with Hades, lifting his gaunt legs, bending his crooked knees, he twirls, he cavorts, he knows no pain, he capers he frisks the music is sprightly a hornpipe a jig a sailor swinging his arms and bobbing his head to the tunes of a bos'n pipe and a tin whistle.

Ω

My father ran across the sand and dove into the warm water, he stretched forward one stalwart arm, then quickly the other, he turned his head to breathe, smiling, gladsome, lithe, he cut through the waves and furrows all grace and strength and welfulness, and I dove next and followed and swam beside him, we were two ships two ditties two calm sleek porpoises steering forward with someplace to go.

vii: Epigraphs. Ovid, *Metamorphoses*, trans. Arthur Golding (1567), 13.898ff.

> John Woolman, *The Journal* (1774), 28th Day, Fifth Month, 1772.
> Homer, *Odyssey*, trans. A. T. Murray (1931), 5.394ff.
> Oppian, *Halieutica*, trans. A. W. Mair (1928), bk. 2.
> Ray Whitley and Gene Autry, "Back in the Saddle Again," (1938)

5: July 1, 2008. Give each man his due. Slightly misremembering *Hamlet*, 2.2.516–17.

5: July 5, 2008. The Oracle at Delphi. "The Oracles at Delphi No Longer Given in Verse," in Plutarch's *Moralia*.

5: July 7, 2008. The Birkenhead Drill. Kipling, "Soldier an' Sailor Too."

10: July 21, 2008. 'Tis Madness. Andrew Marvell, "An Horatian Ode upon Cromwel's Return from Ireland."

10: July 22, 2008. The doctor in Lear. *King Lear*, 4.4.12–15.

11: July 27, 2008. As the fleet left port. The first tune is "Empty Saddles," by Billy Hill. The second, coauthored by Ray Whitley and Gene Autry, became the latter's signature song. Its chorus goes:

> Whoopi-ty-aye-oh
> Rockin' to and fro
> Back in the saddle again.

12: August 11, 2008. Coronis. Ovid, *Metamorphoses* 1.452–567. Pindar, *Third Pythian Ode*. Ovid, *Metamorphoses* 2.602–5.

13: August 16, 2008. Sima Qian, *Records of the Grand Historian*, chap. 6.

14: August 17, 2008. The descent beckons as the ascent beckoned. William Carlos Williams, "The Descent."

16: August 24, 2008. Faraway love. As, for example, in Jaufré Rudel's poem, "Lanquan li jorn son lonc en may" (When the days are long in May): *amor de loing*. Also with apologies to Peire Vidal, "Plus que.l paubres, quan jai el ric ostal," and to the heartfelt translations of Paul Blackburn.

> Heigh ho. From Thomas Lodge, "Rosalind's Description: Like to the Clear in Highest Sphere."

17: September 10, 2008. Sibyl of Cumae. *Aeneid* 6.268ff.

> A workman casts it. Isaiah 40:19.

20: October 20, 2008. Shooting dolphins. Oppian, *Halieutica*, bk. 5.

21: October 24, 2008. Harry. *Henry V*, 4.prologue.

21: November 5, 2008. Acteon. Ovid, *Metamorphoses* 3.138ff.

28: June 5, 2009. Open boat. Remembering Shackleton. The story is admirably told by the ship's captain, W. A. Worsley, who piloted the craft, in *Shackleton's Boat Journey* (1933).

29: June 23, 2009. Bright things. *A Midsummer's Night Dream*, 1.1.148–49.

34: August 3, 2009. The two hours' traffic of our stage. *Romeo and Juliet*, Prologue.12.

34: August 6, 2009. The Oracle of Trophonios. Pausanias, *Description of Greece* 9.39. Mary Hamilton, *Incubation: Or, The Cure of Disease in Pagan Temples and Christian Churches* (1906).

35: August 29, 2009. Eels boiled in broth. From the ballad "Lord Randal," in which the young man visits his sweetheart and returns home to die, poisoned.

35: August 30, 2009. The pestilence comes of three things. Knutsson, *A Litil Boke for the Pestilence*.

36: October 23, 2009. the arrow that flieth by day. *Book of Common Prayer*, no. 91. See no. 90 for threescore and ten.

37: October 27, 2009. The brief trances of the artillery. Shelley, "Hellas."

38: April 16, 2010. How have you known the miseries of your father. *Lear*, 5.3.24.

41: July 9, 2010. Widows. Chaucer, *The Clerk's Tale*.

Let them scratch where it itches. Dante, *Paradiso*, 17.129.

42: July 27, 2010. I will sprinkle clean water upon you. Ezekiel 36:25–26.

43: August 4, 2010. The sea had soaked his heart through. Chapman's rendition of *Odyssey* 5.455–56.

44: September 1, 2010. His ears hear dreadful noises. *Richard III*, 1.4.21ff.

44: September 8, 2010. The eye that mocks a father. Misremembering, slightly, Proverbs 30:17.

Roman law. George Long, *Leges Corneliae*. In: William Smith, *A Dictionary of Greek and Roman Antiquities* (1875), 686–87.

44: September 23, 2010. Go not yet hence. Thomas Nashe, "Fair Summer Droops," in *Summer's Last Will and Testament*. Cf. Coleridge, "Dejection: An Ode."

44: September 28, 2010. Love and the gracious heart. Dante, *Vita Nuova*.

45: October 14, 2010. A great beast. Psalm 104:26.

45: October 21, 2010. This, my Lords. Uttered at the end of speeches, whether in Parliament or court, in Francis Bacon, *History of the Reign of King Henry VII*.

46: November 3, 2010. Hektor. *Iliad* 24.15ff.

46: November 4, 2010. Bones well burnt. Thomas Browne, *Hydriotaphia*.

46: November 5, 2010. Metis. Hesiod, *Theogony* 886–900.

47: November 6, 2010. No thunderbolt. Sophocles, *Oedipus at Colonus* 1659–65.